THE
AMAZON SALES FORMULA

A No Experience Required, Step By Step Instructional Guide To Leverage Private Labeling and Fulfillment By Amazon, To Generate Thousands Per Month In Passive Income.

By Michael D. Marani, M.Ed.

Table of Contents

A Note To the Reader:

Before you read this book, and embark upon this journey, please understand that the information provided is derived from my experience only. It is not to be interpreted in any way, shape, or form as a guarantee that you'll receive similar results. Your results may be better, or your results might be worse. It will come down to what you're willing to put into it. Follow the steps provided in this book, and you'll increase your chances of success, but again, your specific results are in no way guaranteed.

<u>Introduction</u>

Congratulations on taking action. The purchase of this book means you're aspiring for more, and you're willing to do something about it. Before we get started, I'd like to explain how this book should be read, the mindset required on your part to yield the results you're looking for, and who I am. A genuine understanding of the first two components will increase the likelihood that you are successful, and I hope learning some of my story will inspire you. Let's start with introductions.

Who I Am

I am an educator with over 9 years of experience as a teacher, and an additional 2 years as an educational administrator. The difficult part of working in education is the inverse relationship between fulfillment and compensation. I love being an educator. However, I was also born with an entrepreneurial spirit. These two fields clash. I knew I wanted to utilize the entrepreneur in me, so I could subsidize my income and provide the lifestyle I yearned to give my family. Speaking of which, I am a happy husband and father of two.

Not long ago, in order to achieve the lifestyle I wanted without having to give up my career as an educator, I decided to learn about ways to generate multiple streams of passive income: affiliate sites, blogs, app development, writing eBooks, and many more. Each of these items is a legitimate opportunity to generate real income. In fact, I'm currently pursuing each of these methods with real success. The reason I finally moved forward with selling physical products on Amazon is because it really wasn't super complicated. It wasn't, and still isn't, always easy. Although, the concept is pretty simple to understand. Find a product that people will purchase, find a source for that product, send that product to an Amazon warehouse, and watch the money accumulate. Sure this is an oversimplification, but conceptually it is true.

I dabbled, but couldn't honestly call myself a successful entrepreneur. Not until I created my own brand to sell exclusively on Amazon. Within the first two weeks of selling my first product, I was generating thousands of dollars in sales. It only grew from there. This was no accident, and no happy coincidence, it took a ton of hard work and persistence.

My goal is to help every person that reads this book achieve the same success I achieved, but efficiently. I spent a great amount of money taking courses trying to learn the strategies to be successful in the Amazon world. The information that helped create my success was well worth the investment. If only because, I've made it back many times over.

It is also important to acknowledge that if I didn't invest so much of my own money in courses, I would have had more capital to invest in product development. In turn, I could have earned a greater amount of revenue and profit at a faster speed.

The purpose of this book is to provide the right amount of information to take you from having zero experience earning money online to selling thousands of dollars in a relatively short amount of time. I am currently developing a website to offer a course that takes everything in this book into further depth, and includes video tutorials of everything covered and more. Visit **zoniversity.com** if you're interested. Do not feel obligated to use the website. The information in this book encompasses all the information you'll need to achieve success.

Mindset

You're probably not going to like what I'm about to say, and I know this, because I didn't want to hear (or read) it when I was starting out in the Internet sales game. If your mindset is not right, you will not be successful. This book contains specific steps and strategies that brought many others and me real success. If you're not mentally prepared to persist through all the obstacles ahead, you might as well put this book down now, and start working on your mindset.

I attribute a great amount of my successful mindset to Napolean Hill, Dale Carnegie, Tony Robbins, Tim Ferriss, and T. Harv Ecker. If you don't know who they are, I strongly recommend you learn about them first. To avoid going on and on about this topic (because I'm obsessed with this topic), I'll summarize all that I learned with a quote from Henry Ford; "Whether you think you can or you can't, you're right." Some people consider that nonsense. I would argue that if you talk to most successful people, they would agree with it.

How To Read This Book

This book is meant to be utilized as a set of instructions with a hint of motivation, and a strong splash of strategy. The sequencing of this book was very carefully planned. I strongly encourage you to complete the steps as you go. Do not read the book all at once, and then start doing the steps. Start the steps when you start the book, and complete each step as you complete each section. Achieving a high, passive income stream is not easy. The path to it is full of obstacles. However, if you follow the steps provided in this book, it will break down the process into manageable tasks that will move you from a reader of an eBook to an entrepreneur using Amazon to generate thousands of dollars in sales.

The Basics

Reading beyond this point means that you are mentally prepared to begin selling your own private labeled products on Amazon. Moreover, you've accepted that the key to success is to take action. Therefore, you should NOT be reading this book in its entirety before you start taking action. I apologize for the redundancy, but it is extremely important that you allow the sequence of sections in this book to dictate the order of the actions you take.

Before you begin reading and completing the action steps, you'll need to know a little terminology. You'll learn more terms as you continue through the book. However, certain terms are pivotal components of the processes you're about to learn. Therefore, these terms should be discussed right away, so you know what your end result should look like.

Seller Account - is the account that the seller logs into to view their sales data and other related information. It is accessed via **sellercentral.amazon.com**. This may also be referred to as **Seller Central**.

Private Labeling - means that you're hiring a manufacturer and/or supplier to produce multiple units of a certain product. You'll have your logo placed somewhere on the product or the packaging.

Side note, you'd be surprised how many big time, well known brands do this.

FBA - is an acronym for Fulfillment By Amazon. For a nominal fee, Amazon will completely take care of the shipping process for you. This is crucial for two reasons. First, if you truly want your income to be passive having to ship a unit every time an order is placed is a direct contradiction. Second, it is difficult to obtain the option of qualifying for Prime customers.

Prime Customers - are shoppers who pay a fee to receive certain perks, including free two-day shipping. The nice part about this is, the shipping does not cost the seller in anyway. It doesn't earn you any additional profit either, but it opens your product up to Amazon customers who shop so frequently it is worth paying a fee to receive free two-day shipping.

FBA Warehouse - is where you'll send your product units. Later on, you'll learn how to print shipping labels with your seller account. Amazon owns warehouses throughout the country. So, you may have to ship your units to multiple warehouses depending on your packaging. When customers order your product, depending on where they are having the product delivered to, Amazon will automatically determine which warehouse to ship from. This will help customers receive the product quickly, which means you'll be likely to receive positive seller feedback.

Seller Feedback - is the review a customer leaves regarding the service you provided. This feedback is not about the product itself. This is important. If you have too many negative comments, then people won't be willing to purchase from you. By utilizing FBA, you'll likely avoid 90% of potential negative comments.

Customer Reviews - are the reviews a customer leaves about your product. When you're starting out these are the bread and butter of selling your product. Many people won't consider purchasing a product if it receives a significant amount of poor reviews.

Moreover, many people won't consider purchasing a product if it has very few reviews. Soon, you'll learn how to obtain reviews from your customers.

Sourcing Products - is the act of paying a supplier and/or manufacturer to send multiple units to you or a FBA Warehouse.

Now that you have an understanding of some terminology, the paragraph below is your mission statement. Feel free to add to it; make it your own. To me, the purpose of writing this book is so readers can achieve the following:

> **By the conclusion of this book, I will have completed all steps, and have a product under my own brand name live on Amazon. I will be focused on obtaining reviews and increasing sales by utilizing the marketing and email strategies offered in this book. Once I am happy with the sales of my product, I will repeat the steps to start adding additional products to my brand.**

If you're happy with the mission statement, you're ready to move on. Begin by creating your Amazon Seller Central Account. If you are not happy with the mission statement, you have to ask yourself if this is the right book for you. It won't be easy, but I believe that this book will make it as easy as it can be, and regardless of how challenging it is for you, you'll be happy that you did it.

Setting Up Your Seller Central Account

I'm sure you're excited to begin. I'll be brief, and provide the necessary steps to set up your Amazon seller account. As you go through these steps, if you're feeling confused or something doesn't look right contact Amazon seller support. They'll answer any specific questions, and they're pretty quick to respond.

1. Go to sellercentral.amazon.com.

2. Click "Register Now".

3. Choose to Sell as a Professional.

4. Complete information.

    a. Be sure to use an email address that is NOT associated with any other Amazon account.

5. I recommend creating a new email specifically for this Amazon venture.

6. This information can be changed later - so don't sweat it.

7. Legal Name is your name or your company's name.

    a. If you don't have a legal company yet, don't worry. I didn't when I started either. Once you start generating some revenue you can invest in starting an LLC (Limited Liability Company) using LegalZoom.com. This site also provides plenty of educational material if you are unfamiliar with the different types of formal company formats.

8. Make sure you have Fulfillment By Amazon.

9. Click "Continue."

10. **Display Name** - is not important yet, because you haven't identified what type of product you want to sell. Don't worry about this. It can, and most likely will, be changed once you identify what you're going to sell. For now, choose something generic that could work for anything. For example (please don't actually use this), I went with "Quality Priority" for a couple weeks until I narrowed down the category that I was going to sell in.

11. **Address Information** - if you have a company with a separate address use that, or use your home address. I currently use my home address.

12. Click "Save and Continue."

13. **Credit Card Information** - this is when you will be charged $39.99. If you have funds in your account, it will be deducted from those funds. If not, you will need to pay with a debit or credit card. I only had this amount charged on my card once. Every month after that, it would deduct from my earnings.

14. Click "Save and Continue."

15. Follow instructions, and complete the Identity Verification component.

16. Click "Launch Interview Wizard." Remember, if you don't have a company yet that's okay (I didn't either). Answer each question honestly, and you can make necessary updates later.

17. When all the steps are completed, you'll officially have a Seller Account. Be excited! You're one step closer to making it happen. Feel free to look around

Seller Central, but there will be tutorials later in the course. Don't waste too much time. Product research is next, and that is huge.

Product Research:

Finding the right product

Part A

Before we get into the details of how to find the right product to sell, it is important to first focus on what NOT to sell.

Here are some categories I recommend you avoid:

- Clothing

- Collectible Books

- Entertainment Collectibles

- Fine Art

- Gift Cards

⟶ Health & Personal Care

- Industrial & Scientific

- Jewelry

- Luggage & Travel Accessories

- Major Appliances

- Sexual Wellness

- Shoes, Handbags & Sunglasses

- Sports Collectibles

- Textbook Rentals

- Watches

- Wine

In Part B you will develop a table that contains a list of potential products. As you do this, even in the brainstorming component, please keep the following criteria in mind.

How significant is brand awareness?

I wouldn't recommend selling sneakers, because many people will not purchase shoes of a brand they're not familiar with.

How many pieces make up the product?

Remember, the more pieces or the more complicated the product, the more likely it'll break. Moreover, complicated items often require a significant investment.

What is the size of the product?

Remember, the bigger it is the more expensive shipping is. The heavier it is the more expensive the shipping. Expensive shipping equals poor profit margins.

Is the product something you'll be embarrassed to tell people about?

If you feel embarrassed and/or ashamed to tell people about your product, then don't bother. You'll be asking for support and help from your family and friends. If it's a product that you don't want people to know you're selling, you shouldn't sell it.

How much influence does style have?

Please note that this factor won't be as crucial when you start earning some real cash, but unless you have an abundance of wealth, I'm going to assume that you can't afford to customize multiple products multiple times.

The reason why it is important to know these before Part B is you're going to do some number crunching to develop some helpful and informative data. Please keep in mind that if you only look at the data, and you don't consider the factors just stated, you might end up investing in a product that doesn't perform the way you want it to.

Part B

Now that you know what to avoid, and some basic criteria for your product, it is time to start developing a list of potential products.

Here is what you're going to do, step-by-step, for 10 to 20 products. Please be aware that you are about to begin a detail oriented, tedious process. Do not take this process lightly. It is important. However, don't stress. If you find a product that is jumping out at you, because it easily meets all the criteria, you're lucky. Despite my success, I have doubts when I move forward with a new product. I even have doubts about my reorders. These feelings are normal. Be logical and cautious, but don't let fear prevent you from moving forward.

1. Open up Excel, Numbers, or Google Docs (free if you don't have Excel or Numbers). Create one column with a heading titled "Product #" and the column immediately next to it titled "Product Link". Under "Product #" enter "Product #1" all

the way down to "Product #20." Save it as Product Brainstorm List ~ Month. Today's Date.

2. Visit www.amazon.com.

3. Click on Shop by Department.

4. Click on Full Store Directory.

5. Select a category that interests you (please remember the input from "Finding the Right Product" - Part A).

6. Click on Best Sellers.

7. As you browse the products, right click products that look like they have potential and select Copy Link.

8. Go to your "Product Brainstorm List" and paste the link under "Product Link".

   a. Step 7 and 8 are quick. When in doubt copy the link. Don't over think it at this point. There will be a filter process to help you narrow down your results later on. For now, the goal is to find 10 products based on the general criteria provided in Finding the Right Product -Part A.

9. Go back to Amazon and continue this process for one category or multiple until you have a list of 10 to 20 products. Stick to this range. There is no rule that says you can't come back and start this process again if your further filtering process eliminates all 10 to 20 products (which it may).

10. Stand up and stretch out. "Finding the Right Product - Part C" is a doozy.

Part C

Now you have a list of 10 to 20 links that take you to potential products. Your goal here is to develop a table of information that will easily help you narrow down your product list. "Part D" will discuss how to use the information to narrow your list down to 3 or 5 products. Right now, don't get distracted looking at the information. Go into a robotic data input mode where you complete the table using the instructions below without really giving a ton of thought as to what the numbers say. I know that sounds a little strange, but trust me in "Part D" you will have an opportunity to analyze the numbers.

Because I'm a huge fan of number crunching, I'm going to ask that you create another table using Excel, Pages, or Google Docs. This one is going to be a bit more detailed than the last one. Please bear with me.

1. Open up your Product Brainstorm List and copy it.

2. Open up a blank worksheet and paste the Product Brainstorm List.

3. Narrow the Product Link column; it is okay that it doesn't show the whole link.

4. Title the third column "Product Title".

5. Title the 4th through 9th columns "#1 Product Ranking", "#1 Product Reviews" "#2 Product Ranking", "#2 Product Reviews", "#3 Product Ranking", "#3 Product Reviews" respectively.

6. Go back to column three and for each of your products type in the generic title that you think of when you think of that product. Don't use the same exact title provided in the product page. For example a "Thermos Stainless Steel Travel Mug" can be a "travel mug", "coffee mug", or a "travel coffee mug."

7. Search the Product in "#1 Product Title" in the amazon.com search bar.

8. Click on the first product that comes up in the search.

9. Scroll towards the bottom and look next to where it says "Amazon Best Seller Rank" - record that number. Scroll up towards the title of the product and record the number of reviews.

10. Under "#1 Keyword Ranking" type the Amazon Best Seller Rank number you recorded in Step 9.

11. Under "#1 Keyword Reviews" type in the number of Reviews that you recorded in Step 9.

12. Repeat Steps 7 through 11 for all of your products.

When the table is complete you will be able to eliminate some products, and start focusing on your remaining products.

Part D

At this point, you should have a table of 10 to 20 potential products. Each product should have a main keyword along with 3 Product Rankings and 3 Review Quantities. Go through that list, and start eliminating products using the following criteria.

Note - do not actually delete these products. Just add a strikethrough, highlight it red, or in some way denote that these items are not worth pursuing, for now. The reason I say this is, I ended up moving forward with a product I originally eliminated after reanalyzing the data.

Eliminate the product if...

1. it has 2 or more Review Quantities of 1,000 or more.

2. it has Product Rankings over 10,000.

3. it has a Product Ranking sum of 15,000.

4. the product is embarrassing to tell people you're selling.

5. the product brand is a huge factor.

6. the product is very complicated (laptops, engines, washer machines).

7. the product looks heavy or big. This will pay off big time via shipping costs when you're sourcing your product from over seas.

Hopefully, this brought you down to 3 to 5 products. If it brought you down to a quantity lower than 2, no worries keep going. If you're at 1, keep going, but be ready to go through "Finding the Right Product" process another time in case sourcing your product doesn't work smoothly. If you have 0, I hate to say it but you have to go back to "Product Research ~ Part A" and start over. I strongly suggest you do not do it right now. Give yourself credit for going through the process and take a break. If you're stressed tell yourself this line…

"If it were easy, everybody would do it."

Don't get overwhelmed. I went through this process for a total of 13 hours to find my first product. When I final found it, I wasn't even that thrilled about it. I moved forward anyways, and now I look at my Amazon Seller app, and watch the money accumulate (there will be more on that down the road).

If you have narrowed down your list to 3 to 5 products by filtering it using the criteria above, then you are ready to start figuring out how to source your product.

Nice job getting through it!

Additional Research Options

Now that you've been through all four parts of "Finding the Right Product" you may or may not be feeling 100% sure about the product(s) that you're thinking about pursuing. Assuming you're not feeling sure about your potential product (if you are sure, then you're good to go), I have two points I'd like to address in response to these feelings.

First point, on every product I pursued, I was never felt 100% sure that I was making the right choice. Now, I'm not a doctor, but I don't think I'm way off when I say that the mind does funny things when it is time to invest your own money. If you want to make a change in your life you need to accept that no decision is going to be 100% the right decision. You have to be okay with the thought that things WILL go wrong. Success is when you learn from those lessons, and work around them, so they don't prevent you from reaching your goals.

The reality is, I invested a ton of money into making an income via Amazon. I never would have done that if I wasn't mentally prepared to deal with the issues that came up. Go for it! Believe that bumps in the road will not stop you from getting where you want to go.

Second point, below is a list of some resources that help you make a decision. Some of these are pay sites, but they're worth it. I use all of them to help me with my product research, and I recommend you take advantage of them. That said, you could get by with the strategy provided in the "Finding The Right Product" series. In addition to the sites below there is more information on Keyword Research in the section titled "Your Product Is Live! Now What?"

www.fbatoolkit.com - This website will calculate an estimated amount of sales per day based on a ranking you choose. I use it when I find a product with potential. I try to find out how many units I think I'll sell per day if I have a 10,000 ranking, 7,500 ranking, 5000 ranking, 2,500 ranking, and a 1,000 ranking.

www.merchantwords.com - This site is huge for two reasons. One, it tells you how many people are searching your product on Amazon. Two, it often provides a list of other potential keywords. Of the three sites I provide here, merchantwords.com is without a doubt my #1 recommendation.

www.zonspy.com - This website is cool because it was developed by an Amazon seller, who is extremely successful. He developed a site to help automate and expedite his research process. He then made it a subscription site. I recommend this site, but my only reservation is that it can provide too much information. I have often found myself wasting time in analysis paralysis.

I use all three of these sites on a regular basis, and I recommend you do the same. This does not mean you need them, so don't worry about it if you can't afford them.

That said, merchantwords.com is worth canceling cable until you start generating income from your sales.

Use any and all of these sites to help you narrow down your products, or at least give you a second approach to confirm whether or not you are ready to start trying to source a product. You may need to start the "Finding The Right Product" process over. If you need to start over don't become frustrated. This one hurdle separates you from people who do not have what it takes to get to their first sale.

Side note: the first sale is an awesome feeling. Does it mean your rich? Definitely not. Does it officially take you from wantrepreneur to entrepreneur? You bet.

Adaptability - Innovative Ways to Identify Products That Will Sell

Before you move on to sourcing your product, it is important to take a moment to reflect on the research process. I recommended that you write down your thoughts and feelings about this experience while it is fresh in your mind.

This may not be important down the road, but it also could end up being crucial. Therefore, completely worth the time investment. Moreover, this information is available, in one form or another, for everyone. This means you're competing against many people using the same strategy. That statement is a bit scary. Remember, Amazon has so many products that market saturation will be easy to avoid. It is smart however, to develop your own strategy for finding products to sell. Take the strategy I am giving you, and make it your own. Don't underestimate how little changes can make a big difference. I remember a day when I was starting out, and sales hadn't gained momentum, I adjusted the order of the words within a title. I made four sales within an hour of that change. I ended the day with 14 sales, which was a record high at that point. My next highest was six sales. Moral of the story, little changes can make a big difference.

Don't let this section deter you from moving forward with the current strategy. Once you have a couple products up on Amazon, and you've started to generate a consistent cash flow, I strongly recommend you start playing around with your product search process. Adaptability is the key to growing and maintaining a long lasting business, particularly on Amazon.

Before You Source Your Product

If you're not sure what product you're going to end up investing in, then it may be difficult for you to come up with a brand until you have finalized your product (which cannot be finalized until you make an agreement with a supplier). Conversely, if you aren't sure what product you're going to source and sell on Amazon, but you know what category it is going to be in, then you can begin the process of developing your brand before or during the sourcing process.

To shed some light on this subject, an experience I encountered may be helpful. When I was negotiating with suppliers, I was pursuing one particular product, and ordered samples from three suppliers. While I was waiting for my samples to arrive, I identified my brand name and developed my logo (all these steps will be explained next). After receiving my samples, I learned that the amount I was willing to invest would yield low quality products. Therefore, they would not be suitable. It wasn't a big deal. I had multiple products worth sourcing due to my product research strategy. Unfortunately, I wasted about $100.00 on a logo design that I no longer needed. Moral of the story, if money is not yet a plentiful resource for you, then you're going to want to hold off on brand design development until you know for sure what product category you're going to sell.

You might be thinking that you should start the branding process after the sourcing process, but your supplier will ask you for the logo and brand name. You'll want to have them ready, so you can keep the sourcing process progressing. When the right time for you to develop your brand name and logo presents itself, follow the specific steps provided in the next section.

Creating Your Brand

Establishing your brand and brand logo are an essential part of the private labeling process. Additionally, though this can be a bit overwhelming for many, it does not have to be a difficult process. The major thing to think about is the fact that your brand name and logo need to pop.

To me, there are two types of people when it comes to approaching this process. First, you could be a person that loves almost everything you see or hear until, of course, somebody shows you something cooler. You go from one concept to another without any rational reason why one is better than the other, other than the fact that you like it or don't like it. The second type of person can never find the right one. Whether it is the brand name or the logo, this person is always seeking the "perfect" solution.

Side note: Regardless of which person you are, if you do not have self-discipline, then you're going to have a very tough time with this.

I recommend, you limit yourself to no more than 5 days to have a logo and a brand name picked out. I actually give myself 3 days, but I felt bad doing that to you. So, I'll give you two extra days. But honestly, the strategies below will not require 5 days worth of action on your part.

Now that you have your 5-day limit, you're ready to start focusing on finding your brand name. Brainstorm a list of possible brand names. Consider the category that you want to sell in. Remember, that if your brand name is too specific, then you may have a tough time finding your next product. For these purposes, brainstorm and don't worry at all about thinking of bad names. Go for quantity. Follow the steps below to narrow your list down.

1. Find out if your desired brand name is trademarked. To do this check out www.uspto.gov/trademarks/

   a. Do not worry about trademarking your brand name, and do not worry about starting an official corporation at this point. You will be able to sell on amazon.com before you have to start your company. I didn't do any of this until I started making real money. Some people will say you're taking a risk by doing this. Honestly, those people might be right. My counter to this is that when you start selling a decent volume of products the chances of anything going terribly wrong will be so minimal that it should not be anything that prevents you from moving forward. When you get to the point where you're going to make things official, check out zoniversity.com for help on this process.

2. Find out if your desired brand name domain is available. If not, move on to another name. For example, if you want a brand name called "Awesome Forks". Then you should check and see if www.AwsomeForks.com is available. If you don't know how to do this go to godaddy.com,

and search for your potential domain. If it isn't available, then refer back to your brainstorm list.

   a. Side note: I only consider domain names that end with .com. If it isn't available with a .com ending, then I don't want it. Some may disagree, but I recommend avoiding the other options.

3. If you have multiple brand names that made it through this filter process, compile a list of your remaining potential brand names, and have as many people as possible pick the one they like the best. Don't give them too much information; have them select their top three. Pick the one that is liked the most.

4. Once you have the brand name, purchase the domain right away. I use GoDaddy.com to do this, but other reliable companies are hostgator.com and bluehost.com. I've used all three, and they're all reputable and reliable. It comes down to personal opinion.

5. Start thinking of your logo. If you're close to the 5-day time limit (and you're limited on funds) check out http://99designs.com/logo-design/store. This link will bring you to a page with predesigned logos that you can purchase for $99.00 (this is a very reasonable price). Within 24 hours your selected design will have your brand name inserted into it, and you'll have your logo.

   a. Side note: I recommend you stick to simple designs. The more complicated and intricate the design, the more expensive it will be to print on a mass scale.

b. Remember, you can always change your logo and brand name. Will it cost you extra money down the road? Yes. Will the amount be so steep that it will cause you to delay this process, and allow yourself to waste a month or more on it? No, definitely not. Get your brand name, get your logo, and move one step closer to selling physical products by sourcing your product.

Obtaining a UPC

When you add a product to sell on Amazon, you'll be prompted to add a UPC (Universal Product Code). Some might say that you don't have to. From my experience, it eliminates any potential labeling issues that can cause serious inventory delays. I go to www.codeupc.net to purchase my UPC. Their prices are reasonable, and every transaction I've had with them has been a positive experience. Therefore, they gave me no reason to try elsewhere.

The greater the amount of unique codes you purchase, the lower the unit cost will be. For the purposes of our mission of selling on Amazon, for now, we only need to purchase one UPC, which would then be copied onto a hanging tag, which is often used as a price tag in physical stores. The bar code graphic will come with your purchase, along with the number, and will only be needed for your hanging tag. The UPC will be requested when you add your listing.

The only area of confusion is whether or not this process is required for Amazon sellers. The answer is, not always. Due to the uncertainty and potential for mistakes when your product units arrive at the Amazon warehouse(s), I recommend you ensure that a UPC and barcode are included somewhere on the outside of your packaging.

In addition to this process, you're also going to elect to have Amazon label your product's SKU (Stock Keeping Unit) code. This is a specific code that Amazon uses for their systems. They charge you $.20 per unit. For that reason, I recommend you send in a max of 300 units for your first time around.

This may mean you'll have some boxes of product stacked somewhere in your house or office. It's worth the space use at home, considering Amazon will deduct the 20%, or $.20 per unit, directly from your compensation amount. You can find information about your compensation amount in Seller Central (a.k.a. Seller Account).

To reiterate, having your UPC and your Amazon SKU code is a bit redundant. The redundancy in this case, is necessary. It will prevent any lost product units or incorrectly categorized units. If you want to take your chances and save some capital, then go ahead, but know that it is not my recommendation.

Sourcing Your Product

Preparing to Source

Before shifting focus onto sourcing your product, it is important to make sure you are prepared both mentally and organizationally. Lets start with the mental aspect.

This is the first phase where you are vulnerable to the work of others. In other words, the pace that you have been able to keep up until this point has rested entirely on you. Sourcing your product puts you in a position where you are waiting for somebody else to provide you with information. This process will be time consuming. I remember the first I talked to potential supplier at midnight (because they're 12 hours ahead) via Skype.

Here is the other thing you need to be mentally prepared for; you'll be negotiating with people. This means it is going to take a ton of patience and persistence, while communicating with different suppliers, until you find the appropriate terms.

This is the phase that I thought was going to drive me to quit. Night after night, I would be exhausted trying to negotiate an agreement that would allow me to test a product without having to purchase 1,000 units.

Don't be intimidated by this, you only have to go through this process once per supplier. I only communicate with three suppliers. When I want to test the market for another product, I throw it out to my suppliers. If they don't offer what I'm looking for, they connect me with others. I have great relationships with my suppliers, which makes the negotiating process extremely smooth. You'll get to this point, but it does take time.

Do not quit. You'll find a supplier who can provide you with the product you want with reasonable terms. If you start feeling like you're going to quit, remind yourself that the reason why you'll be successful is because you're willing to endure and persist in a very time consuming, stressful process. When your product is selling on Amazon, and your friends are asking you, "What is stopping people from selling the same product as you?" I suggest you smile, and say nothing. Even though you know that finding a product that sells is no easy task, and sourcing that product is even harder. Don't be the person who quits, then looks back asking yourself, "What if?" Keep pushing. The light at the end of the tunnel is well worth the hard work. Once you find your supplier, you'll be one step closer to earning passive income.

Organizing and Strategizing

Before you start your negotiations with suppliers, you need to be ready to receive all the information in an organized way. To do this, you need to set up another spreadsheet and some folders. View the instructions below:

1. On the far left column add the following categories in this order.

    a. Company Name

    b. Product

    c. Contact

    d. Contact Email

    e. Company Mailing Address

    f. Minimum Order Quantity (No Logo)

    g. Minimum Order Quantity (Logo)

    h. Unit Price

    i. Shipping Cost

    j. Payment Types Accepted

2. Create a folder for each company that you're regularly communicating with. Don't feel the need to do this for suppliers that you are only in early stages of discussion. Once you start discussing specific numbers (i.e. prices, order quantities, etc.), create a folder for that supplier. Each folder will be utilized to contain any files (images, invoices, etc.) from each supplier. All of these folders should be within another folder titled "Supplier Information".

3. Place your spreadsheet in your "Supplier Information" folder (but do not place it in any specific supplier folder).

This process is more important than you think, you'll end up being in 7 or 8 on-going negotiations that occur via Skype or email (don't worry we'll discuss this in a later section), and it is easy to start confusing which supplier is offering which product under what specific terms.

Other than organization purposes, this will also serve as a great reference when you start researching product 2 and 3 (and 4 and 5 and 6 and 7).

Determining Your Price

Though you do not have your product live at this point, it is important to have an idea as to what price your product will eventually be. This needs to happen before you negotiate, so you know that the price you pay makes sense. To determine this, you need to look at two primary factors:

1. What are the products you'll be competing with going for?

2. What price allows you to generate an adequate profit?

Let's first focus on the competition. One thing I learned, very quickly, is that I could have the best product page, with amazing images and a description page that reads like informative poetry, but if my product wasn't priced appropriately chances are customers would go with a different option. That is not to say that you can't price your product higher than the competition (which is not a great strategy when trying to break into a market). How much higher can be the difference between converting your traffic into sales 20% of the time or 5% of the time.

Moral of the story, if you're product stands out, because it is so outrageously expensive, then chances are you're not going to be selling many units. Likewise, if you're product is inexplicably lower in price, than the rest of your competition, you may need to increase the price to avoid coming off as a low quality product. Follow the steps (for each of your potential products) below to help get a better understanding of what your pricing strategy might look like.

1. Create a spreadsheet with two columns. Title the first column "Product #" and the second "Price".

2. Under "Product #" type in "Product 1", "Product 2", "Product 3", and so on until you've hit the total number of products on page 1 and page 2 once you've searched your product.

3. Please note that you should NOT include any of the sponsored products that show up on the pages.

4. Under "Price" begin listing the price for each product. Continue to do this for all of your products.

5. Find the average of all the product prices.

6. Find the average of the products that most closely match your potential product.

7. Keep these numbers clearly labeled (so you know the difference later), and be ready to refer to them when you're trying to calculate your potential price, which will be covered next.

8. Save the file as "_____*Product* Pricing Strategy". Instead of using the product name, use the keyword(s) you typed into the search bar. For example, "Ice Cub Tray" Pricing Strategy.

Before moving on to the Amazon Profit Calculator, please be aware that the longer you're willing to break even on products, the better position you'll have for long term gains. When I first started selling, I wanted profits right away, and I got them. I realize now, that for that particular product, I positioned myself in a way that quickly hit a ceiling. This is a slow and complex process. You may need to earn some profit, so you can invest it in additional inventory. Ultimately, do what you have to do, but be aware that you should factor in 100 units that you'll willingly give away.

I understand that thought is scary, but it will pay off by allowing you to break into the market, and start getting consistent sales with a more profitable price.

To determine what price allows you to earn a specific profit, login into your sellercentral.amazon.com account, then follow the link below, and use the instructions below to help you complete the calculator correctly.

https://sellercentral.amazon.com/gp/fba/revenue-calculator/index.html

1. Once you've gone to the site above, type in the general name of the product you used to search your competition's product pricing.

2. Select one that resembles something you're going to shoot for. Don't worry if you're not sure what your product is going to look like. This will give you a ballpark idea of the profit you can earn per product.

3. Under "Amazon Fulfillment" type in an "Item Price" that you're considering based on the average you calculated in your "Product Pricing Table."

4. Still under "Amazon Fulfillment", across from "Inbound Shipping" type in 1.00. This may not be exact, but it's in the range if you follow the criteria for selecting a product (and avoiding certain products).

5. Go a little bit lower across from "Prep Service," type .20 into that space. This is the cost per item that Amazon charges to put an Amazon bar code sticker onto your product. This is worth the money; it ensures that your product will be labeled correctly (and it is one less thing that can take up a significant amount of time).

6. Click the "Calculate" button. The green number at the bottom is your "Margin Impact," which means the amount of money per unit that Amazon will compensate you for selling. Be aware that this is not your profit. You have to factor in how much you paid for your product units, and the cost to ship them to your location. Use the formula below to help:

   a. **Margin Impact - (Product Unit Cost + (Total Shipping Cost/Total Units)) = Profit Per Unit**

7. Play with the calculator by adjusting the "Item Price". Determine your break-even price, your market entry price (which could be the same as your break even price), and your goal price. Consider these numbers as you negotiate with your potential supplier, but be aware that your profit margins will become much more appealing as you become a regular purchaser from a supplier.

8. Repeat this process for all products that you're planning on negotiating for.

Negotiating With Suppliers

Here we are. You're organized, and you're mentally prepared. You're ready to take on one of the most challenging parts of this process. Remember, eventually you will land on terms your comfortable with, and you will have your own product live on Amazon. Here are the steps:

1. Go to alibaba.com and create an account. I am not providing specific instructions because the site makes it pretty easy.

    a. Note: it is not required to have a company name when you fill out the information, but some suppliers may disregard you if you don't have one. Do not worry if you don't, because there are plenty of suppliers. I'm often overwhelmed at how many responses I get (which I will address below).

2. Now that you have your account set up, start searching each of the products that you have decided to move forward with.

    a. Note: You want to have two to three products, because I'm suggesting a strategy that encourages multiple organized negotiations. This way, you can select a product that meets your demand criteria, but also meets the best terms that you can afford. This may make things a bit more difficult, but it will save you a ton of time if one of the products turns out not to be available in a way that meets your needs.

3. For each of your product searches scan through the suppliers.

    a. Note: Utilize the filters on the left if you have certain specifications that you'd like to meet (i.e. a US supplier vs. a Chinese supplier). After you assess your options, select the top three to five suppliers depending on how fast you want to move this process along. Be aware that selecting five will make organization even more essential. If you struggle with spreadsheets (creating, maintaining, etc.) then you may want to contact three suppliers. Remember, 3 suppliers per product. If you have 3 products, you're contacting 9 suppliers and keeping them organized.

4. For each product supplier that appears to fit your needs, or comes the closest, press the "Contact the Supplier" button. Utilize the template below to help guide your message.

    a. Dear *insert name of salesperson here,* (can be found next to "To:" under your email address).

    I'm contacting you because my market research indicates that the *insert product name here* has earning potential. At your convenience, please contact me so we can discuss your market test order MOQ (Minimum Order Quantity), private label/OEM (Original Equipment Manufacturer) options, and shipping options.

Please know that I prefer to start with a smaller order of, *insert number of units if less than 1,000,* to confirm that my research proves correct. I'm looking to create an ongoing, mutually beneficial business relationship. If you prefer to contact me via Skype feel free to add my username, *insert Skype username,* as a contact.

Thank you, and I look forward to hearing from you.

5. Before you send the message, be sure to match the number of units identified in your message in the box titled "Quantity Needed."

6. Lastly, do NOT check the box next to "Recommend matching suppliers if this supplier doesn't contact me on Message Center within 24 hours". Doing so will create a situation where you might find yourself losing track of your suppliers, and you may not being able to decipher who is offering what product, at what price, under what terms.

7. The hardest part.) - Now you wait for the responses.

A few points to consider while you wait for your responses. Be aware that different countries are in different time zones, which means if you live in the US and you're negotiation with a Chinese supplier, then you need to be prepared for one and/or two things. Either the negotiations will be conducted 100% via email, which is very slow; and/or via Skype, which means very late nights since they're 12 hours ahead of the US. Despite this, I recommend you do the bulk of your negotiation via Skype, because it is the quickest approach.

Secondly, be sure to obtain the information from the table you created:

Company Name

Product

Contact

Contact Email

Company Mailing Address

Minimum Order Quantity (No Logo)

Minimum Order Quantity (Logo)

Unit Price

Shipping Cost

Payment Types Accepted

This will help guide your negotiations. Remember, these suppliers want your business. Don't be afraid to request an adjustment to the numbers to better meet your needs. Before you attempt this, see what the other suppliers are saying. This will help give you a realistic sense of how close you are to either making a deal or looking elsewhere, or at other products.

Third, a lot of suppliers can offer decent prices on low quantities such as 100 to 300 units depending on the product. Even if the product page states that the minimum order quantity (MOQ) is 1,000 or 3,000 units. You'll notice that many suppliers often require larger MOQs when you want to add your logo. This is totally normal, and there are ways around this.

For example, one of the products I currently sell originally did not have the logo on the actual product. Instead, I paid for 5,000 hanging tags (that I got designed, which you'll learn about after negotiations). The tags cost me $160.00 on top of my order. This saved me a ton of money, because it allowed me to avoid paying for the cost of printing the logo directly onto the product. This is okay to do at first. If you were selling your item in a brick and mortar, I might not recommend this approach. Because your customers are Internet shoppers, they are comfortable making purchases based on images, and these images can include your logo in the top left (or any where you think makes sense). Be prepared to get creative during your negotiations.

Fourth, shipping is expensive. I have a couple products that cost me more to ship then to purchase. You can try and avoid this by negotiating with US suppliers, but in my experience the unit costs tend to be higher and therefore, even things out. The one benefit of US suppliers is shipping is often quicker, which is great because you do not want to run out of stock. Staying on top of your inventory is a priority once you're live. Shipping will be discussed later. If you have questions, do not panic.

Fifth and finally, the two ways I send payments are PayPal and Western Union. I prefer PayPal, because there is a bit more security if something were to go wrong. However, Western Union's fee can be waived if you pay via your bank account, rather than a credit card. If you have to pay with a credit card, which I definitely did, you can occasionally find a promo code online to save you money on the payment fee. To clarify, when I say a bit more security with PayPal, I mean that if something were to go wrong with your order, there is a chance you could obtain some of the money you used to make the purchase. If you use Western Union, once your funds are deducted they're gone forever.

Shipping Your Product Units To You First

At this point, you've found a sample that meets your expectations. If not, I suggest you focus more on receiving product samples, before you start worrying about shipping hundreds of units. If you're ready to order your product, then you need to determine the best way to ship your items. When I encountered this situation for the first time, I was very anxious. I wanted to have my units in the FBA warehouse as soon as possible. If this is you, then you want to have your units shipped via air not sea freight. Sea freight takes longer, but can save you money if your order is thousands of units. I'm going to assume that you are not ordering more than 1,000 units for your first few orders. If I'm mistaken, and you are ordering over 1,000 units, then check out zoniversity.com to find more resources on how to go about shipping via sea freight.

Shipping was one stage I underestimated. I remember asking myself, "How hard could it be?" Order it, and they will come. My assumption was incorrect. You need to discuss the method of shipping with your supplier. Therefore, you need to have a plan as to how you're going to receive your items. This can be done in many ways. You can have your supplier forward your units to a port nearby, you can hire a US based forwarder to export them from the place of origin to the US, or you can ask the supplier what shipping options they provide. They'll definitely be able to provide this for you. If they can't, you may want to look elsewhere. The only issue with asking your supplier to use their shipping account to ship your product units is, that they control the information. Who is to say that the supplier isn't adding on an extra $100.00? This is where you have to do your due diligence. Take the following approach with each supplier you negotiate with:

1. Ask your supplier what the weight of each master carton is, and what the dimensions are.

2. Ask your supplier for the exact address.

3. Ask your supplier to provide you with a quote for your units including shipping. If they ask you if you have a preference, then respond saying that you would like the most affordable option.

4. Contact logisticsplus.net. Use the weight and dimension information that your supplier provided along with the supplier address to help provide you with an accurate quote.

5. Choose the most affordable option.

6. Communicate this choice with your supplier.

Two things about the above steps. First, you need to know where you're going to have the units delivered. To expedite the process, since your order isn't going to be huge, I suggest you have them shipped to your house, and then ship them to the FBA warehouse(s).

Second, some people will disagree with only seeking two options for shipping. However, I'm a firm believer that at times too many options can lead to analysis paralysis. Chances are there is no shipping company out there that will dramatically beat a price of a competitor. You're obtaining the other quote to make sure your supplier isn't trying to pull a fast one on you. To this day, I still use my supplier's shipping options. Could I possibly save $50 or $100 if I looked hard enough? Maybe. But, I honestly value my time more than I value that money. If you disagree, Google the term "international shipping companies", then do research, and obtain more quotes.

Above it was mentioned that your first order should be to your house. I say this because you don't have a longstanding relationship with your supplier. You have to keep them honest. Open up the cases when you receive them, and check your product. Make sure that your units meet your expectations. If more than 1% of your units are faulty or not cutting it, then let your supplier know. Please be aware that there isn't much you can do about that particular order, but they'll be sure not to slack when they're packing your next order, They will know you're looking.

Remember, suppliers are companies made up of people. Don't assume that everybody is working as hard as they can at all times. You may have to provide some motivation by making it clear you will have to take your business elsewhere if the issue is not resolved. Moreover, if 5% or more of your units are faulty or not acceptable, you should only send the acceptable ones into the warehouse. Politely demand that the supplier send you the same 5% or more of acceptable replacement products. If not, cut your ties, and look for another supplier.

If the paragraph above gave you a panic attack, then I sincerely apologize. I'm giving you a worst-case scenario, which I've never personally encountered. However, I know other sellers that have. It wouldn't be right if I didn't give you a fair warning.

In order to prevent this risk, I urge you to ask for approximately ten pictures, before they send the products to you. Do not pay your final installment until you see each of those pictures, and you're happy with them. Once you pay your suppliers 100% of the cost, you are officially at their mercy. Don't panic. These companies want to make their customers happy, because they're hoping for future orders.

A quick side note: You can negotiate the terms of how much you pay for each installment, and when you pay, but the standard is to pay 30% of the total (including shipping if the you're utilizing the supplier) before they start manufacturing the product, then the remaining 70% after you see your pictures, but BEFORE they ship them to you. You can try to negotiate terms that allow to you pay a certain percentage after you receive your product.

In all honesty, it's unrealistic for a first time buyer to receive an agreement other than the 30/70 split. If this makes your uncomfortable, I recommend you take advantage of alibaba.com, and only associate with highly qualified and seasoned companies. Do so at your own risk. Sometimes the little supplier, or the new supplier, is more flexible on price and other services.

Preparing For Amazon

Developing Your Product Title

Before you delve deep into this content, there needs to be a couple of disclaimers and/or items of caution. First, Amazon changes their rules constantly, so the specifics provided in this section may become outdated then reinstated a few times over. Don't panic. Some rules of thumb will also be provided in addition to specifics, so you can adapt to any changes Amazon may or may not throw at you. Second, the specifics will bring you a title that is long and, what many might consider, ugly. Moreover, some might say a long title will turn customers off. Before providing a formula to help you develop your title, it is important to explain the reasoning behind the title.

Like Google, Amazon has an algorithm that they revise, update, and utilize to sort out how products appear when a specific keyword is searched. For example, when an Amazon browser searches for "magnetic wristband" a certain amount of products will show up on page one, then page two, then page three etc. If you have a short title that does not include commonly searched keywords, your product is less likely to show up on a low numbered page. A short title minimizes the chances that somebody will type in a keyword that exists within it.

On the other hand, if you create a keyword rich title that contains many characters you're increasing the chances that somebody will search a keyword that exists within your title. This creates more opportunities for potential customers to find your product. If you convert those shoppers into customers at a rate of 20% or greater, you'll start to see your product climb among the keywords included in your title. It becomes a cyclical effect. The more people who find your product, the more customers buy your product, which generates more money for Amazon. This encourages them to place your product front and center, or in this case, high up in the page rank.

Please do not misinterpret the message above. There are plenty of other factors within Amazon's algorithm that determine where your product will be ranked when somebody searches a keyword. Some of these factors are reviews, both verified reviews and unverified reviews, conversion rate, outside traffic, keywords within the page, and many unknowns. These will all be discussed later on when you have your product live.

Until then, stay focused on developing a strong, effective product page by starting with the product title. Use the formula below to guide your product title development. Before you do, here are some rules of thumb to think about if Amazon starts changing things up. You want your title to include as many keywords as possible in the most natural sounding way possible.

In other words, don't list keywords one after another. Make it flow, but do so in a way that is keyword rich. Also, you want the primary keyword listed in the very beginning. For example, "Magnetic Wristband" would be the first words in your title if you were selling a magnetic wristband. Soon after, try to include the word free. For example, Magnetic Wristband - Includes a FREE eBook. I suspect that Amazon will eventually not permit this. Until they say stop, I suggest you also include some sort of price reduction language. For example, "Magnetic Wristband - Includes a FREE eBook

- Price Reduced For A Limited Time." The last rule of thumb, before providing the specific formula, is that you must not underestimate the power of a word within the title.

Here are two example stories to support that previous statement. On Labor Day, I updated wording within my title from "Price Reduced For A Limited Time" to "Labor Day Price Cut Available While Supplies Last". My sales that day sold 400% of my daily average for that particular product. The following day, I adjusted the wording to "Labor Day Price Cut Extended Through Today." My sales were 300% of the daily average. Lastly, to give more evidence that a small change can make a big difference, when I moved my "Free eBook" offer from the end of the title to right after the product's primary keyword, my sales average doubled when comparing the first month with the old format and the following month with the new format. Needless to say, tweaking the words until you hit a solid conversion rate is an absolute necessity. Utilize the formula below to help you get started. For now, type your title into some sort of word document.

Primary Keyword - Something offered for FREE - Price Reduction language - descriptive keywords that address quality - descriptive keywords that provide feature - top of the line keyword - this keyword is perfect for related keywords - Ideal for a couple more related keywords - one year unlimited warranty.

Let me translate this with an example:

Magnetic Wristband - Includes a FREE eBook - Price Cut Available For A Limited Time - High Quality, Durable Yet Comfortable Tool - Top Of The Line Carpenter

Accessory When Using Power Tools - Quickly and Safely Hammer With Nails Always Easily Accessible - Whether You Use Kobalt Tools or Milwaukee Tools This Is The Perfect Product For Your Tool Kit - One Year Unlimited Warranty

There is more to this title than you might notice at first glance. Review the breakdown of keywords and monthly searches (according to merchantwords.com) to see how this title will increase the chances that a potential customer will find this product.

"Magnetic Wristband" searched 5,000 times

"Tool" searched 1,100,000 times

"Carpenter Accessory" searched 16,500 times

"Power Tools" searched 5,650,000 times

"Kobalt Tools" searched 770,000 times

"Milwaukee Tools" searched 760,000 times

"Tool Kit" searched 217,000 times

Now, one might argue that these keywords, with the exception of the "Magnetic Wristband", are pointless, because people aren't looking for a magnetic wristband if they search for a power tool. My response is simply this; I agree. If they are searching for a power tool then they are most likely searching for power tools. However, if they are searching for a power tool then they most likely could use a magnetic wristband. Moreover, the person that is searching for a power tool may not even realize they need a magnetic wristband until they see one. Lets hope they see yours.

This argument could be brought a step further. Think about an experience when shopping at Target. How many times have you gone into Target looking for one thing, and come out with another?

If your answer is zero, good for you. You are extremely self-disciplined. Fortunately for sellers, most people do not keep their blinders on, and often realize they have a need for something when they see the item/s that present a solution to their need.

Lets end this section with a motto to guide your product title development.

"Be the solution to the problems people know they have, and to the problems they don't know they have."

Developing Your Key Product Features

The Key Product Features are the bullet points listed under the Product Title. This is your chance to sell the product. Moreover, this is the section to focus on explaining to potential customers why they should purchase the product. Do not worry about keywords here. When people read this information, they're looking to have questions answered. Your job is to anticipate those questions, and address them in the Key Product Features. Here are some common concerns that potential customers may consider before purchasing your product:

1. What if I receive the product and don't like it? If I return it, will I have to pay for shipping?

2. Will this product be effective? If so, what specific problems will it solve?

3. Is this product safe? Will it damage any related products?

4. Why should I pick this product when there is a similar product $3.00 cheaper?

5. What is the product made of?

6. How many pieces and/or components will I receive?

Understand that these are guiding questions. I don't want to give you a specific template, because this is your chance to stand out. If you're looking for specific samples visit amazon.com and view "Key Product Features" for best sellers within your category. The other factor to consider when developing these features is your own experience as a shopper. Before you purchase a product, what are some of the concerns that you have? Those combined with the questions above should help you develop some sellable and honest product features. View the steps below to start inputting your Key Product Features.

Here is a list of step-by-step instructions to input your product description onto your product page:

1. Open up some type of word document (Microsoft Word, Pages, etc.).

2. Type your features using the guiding questions above (unlike the Product Description, no HTML is necessary).

3. Copy the entire description.

4. Log into your sellercentral.amazon.com account.

5. Click on "Inventory" towards the top left.

6. Click on "Manage Inventory."

7. Go down to "Actions" and click on the down arrow.

8. Click on "*Edit D*etails."

9. Click on the "*D*escription" tab.

10. Paste your bullets one at a time in each space next to Key Product Features.

11. Click "Save and Finish."

Creating Your Product Description

You should view your product description as your opportunity to convince potential customers that your product is the better option compared to all of the competition. To do this, there is a formulaic approach, but please be aware that the goal here is to stand out. Take some time to get creative and figure out how you can differentiate yourself from the competition. Follow the guidelines below to get started.

Assume that you will have to tweak whatever you first come up with. Unless you're averaging unit sale's conversion rates over 30%, you should always be looking for those minor adjustments you can make to improve your conversion rate. In this case, your conversion rate represents the amount of unique shoppers that purchased your product out of the amount of total unique shoppers that visited your product page.

To clarify, and I will delve deeper into how to interpret the data later one, but your unit sale's conversion rate should be over 20%. You might be asking why is it 20%

as opposed to 25% or 15%, and I can only provide an answer based on my experience. I view the unit sale's conversion rate as the mount that holds your page rank in place. If you have a volatile and often low unit sale's conversion rate, you're likely going to see your product bounce up and down a page, and quite possibly bounce from one page to another. I've noticed, over time, that reviews help stabilize this movement. In other words, the greater amount of reviews you have, the more stable your product page will be when somebody searches your primary keywords.

Side note: do not assume that lowering your price is always the solution. I've lowered some of my prices, increased other prices, and very often there does not appear to be a change. The only circumstances in which I noticed a real change in the conversion rate is when I dramatically decrease the price, but that also means I dramatically decreasing my profit margin. Moral of the last three paragraphs is, take your time developing your product page, and be ready to adjust.

If you're nervous about developing your own description page, go to fiverr.com and search "amazon product page", select somebody with reviews both high in quality and quantity. You can hire somebody to develop your page for $5 to $50. Regardless, you should still be prepared to make minor adjustments to this page. Here are the guidelines to help you develop your product description.

Product Description Guidelines

1. Start with a bold title that clearly states the problem your product solves.

2. Add a bulleted list with a title above it that states something like "Looking for product x, but want to avoid these common problems?" Then add a bulleted list directly under the title that provides all the problems customers of your competition will encounter, but that they won't encounter with your product. If you're not sure what problems your competition's customers may encounter, read your competition's negative reviews. They'll tell you plenty of problems that occur with their product.

3. Add a second bulleted list with a title that states something similar to " Want an effective and efficient product x to get the job done?" Then add a bulleted list directly under the title that includes all the special features of your product. If you're not sure what features to mention look at your competition's positive reviews, and identify what people like about the product.

4. Then add one bonus after another as separate lines in bold. For example:

   a. *Free eBook included with purchase.*

   b. *1 Year Unlimited Warranty - No Questions Asked!*

5. Finally, you can add your "call to action" with something like "Click the "Add to Cart Button" before we're sold out!

Now before moving onto to the specific formatting of the product description, I want to make it completely clear that I am not, in any way, suggesting that you write anything that is untrue. What I am suggesting is that you do whatever you can to highlight your product's strengths while emphasizing the problems of others. Follow that up with a bonus, and a risk avoidance strategy (the warranty) right before the call to action. This can greatly increase your chances of converting a shopper to a customer.

The last thing you should keep in mind is that Amazon always seems to be changing the rules. This is fine, but it can be a bit annoying at times. You'll occasionally have to make a few adjustments to make sure that you're in compliance with the rules. When I started selling my first product, I included all sorts of html code that enabled me to create cool looking product descriptions. Amazon has since changed the html code that they allow. Currently, without any sort of html code, your description will be one solid paragraph, even if you type it in with spacing. View the guide below to learn about the only html that is allowed at this time. Please be aware that I have no business writing html (which is a code used to design websites) so if you have no idea what it is or how to use it, don't panic. I'll explain all you need to know.

Currently, the only forms of acceptable html are the following:

<b></b>

<p></p>

If you want to use a bold font, and you will for titles, special bonuses, and other important information, you'll need to put <b> before the text you'd like to make bold. After you've entered the text that you want to be bold close it with </b>. The last code will indicate the next words you type will not be bold. If you don't include the last piece of code, then you're entire description will be bold. You don't want that.

If you want separate paragraphs, you'll need to add <p> at the beginning of the paragraph and </p> at the end.

Lastly, if you'd like a space from one statement to the next, you'll need to add <br>. This code stands for page break, which is one line of space.

To be completely transparent, I need to explain that I'm in no way an html expert, and if you're having a difficult time writing your product description because of the formatting, then you should Google the term "html code help", from there helpful resources (way more helpful than me) will be available.

Here is a list of step-by-step instructions to input your product description to your product page:

1. Open up some type of word document (Microsoft Word, Pages, etc.).

2. Type your description using the guideline above. Be sure to include the html discussed above as well.

3. Copy the entire description.

4. Log into your sellercentral.amazon.com account.

5. Click on "Inventory" towards the top left.

6. Click on "Manage Inventory."

7. Go down to "Actions" and click on the down arrow.

8. Click on "Edit Details."

9. Click on the "Description" tab.

10. Paste your content in the empty box next to "Product Description."

11. Click "Save and Finish."

You're done. Check that task off the list. Be proud of yourself. Move on to the next one!

Setting Up Your Product Page

So you're anxiously awaiting your product's arrival, so you can assess the quality, and forward those items to the FBA Warehouse (which will be discussed very soon). While you're waiting you have plenty to do. You need to begin developing your product page, but before you can do this you need to properly select the category. Follow the instructions below. Please remember not to stress to intensely on this project as everything you do can be adjusted, revised, and completely restarted if need be.

1. Log into your "Seller Central" account (sellercentral.amazon.com).

2. Click on "Inventory."

3. Press the "Add a Product" button.

4. Press the "Create A New Product" button - you're doing this because you're the first one selling your brand. Therefore, if you were to search it in the Amazon database nothing would come up. This will give you an edge when people find your product and visit your product page.

5. Start selecting the categories that best match your product. This process may take a couple of attempts because you want to be able to categorize your product as specifically as possible.

6. After you have either found your exact type of product, or have come as close as possible, you're ready to start developing your page. This portion will automatically begin once you're done selecting your category information. Follow the steps below to go through this.

7. It is stated above, but it is worth repeating, anything you type in can be changed. In fact, it should be changed from time to time. Later on, you'll read about tweaking your product page, and viewing the impact it makes on your conversion rate. Please be aware that Amazon updates their process quite a bit, so there may be a section here or there that isn't required at this moment, but may become required in the future. If you're attempting to enter information now, and something is required that isn't explained below, go with your instinct. If you're uncomfortable with that, you can always contact Seller Central Support.

8. Copy and paste the Product Name into the appropriate section.

9. Enter your brand name for "Manufacturer."

10. Scroll towards the bottom of the page and enter in your "UPC" code.

11. Move onto the "Offer" information by either clicking the "Next" button or just clicking on the "Offer" tab.

12. Scroll to "New" next to "Condition."

13. Enter your price. This is the price that is often crossed out next to another price in red (more on the red price in a moment). This price is still very important. You won't be charging your customers this price, but part of your commission that Amazon charges you will be calculated based on this number. You'll want to find a number that is higher than the price you're planning on selling at, but not too high that it hurts your profit margin. I often adjust this number to see how it will impact my conversion rate. Whatever number you land on will likely be changed multiple times in the near future. Don't take too much time pondering.

14. Set the "Sale Price" to the amount that you're going to be collecting from customers. This is the number posted in red next to the number that's crossed out. This is the amount that customers will actually pay (plus shipping if they're not Amazon Prime members). If you're new to this, you should be starting off with an extremely below market price. Your initial goal is to gain some traction, and earn some reviews (more on this later). Again though, whatever price you pick can be changed easily. So don't waste time worrying about it. Pick something, and move on. Make today's date the "Sale Start Date" and at least two years from now the "End Date."

15. Assuming your product is being sold in units of one, type the number 1 next to "Quantity."

16. Next to "Shipping Method" make sure you select that you want Amazon to handle the shipping. This is the FBA option. If you want passive income this is a necessity. If you want to be able to sell to Amazon

Prime Members, where there is a 2-day shipping guarantee, then this is a necessity.

17. Press "Next" and upload your images. Use all 9 options. If you want people to pay you for a product, then it is fair to offer them as many angles as possible.

18. Press "Next" and move onto the "Description." Copy and past each bullet that you want in your "Key Product Features" space. Utilize each space provided. Take your time on these. People read these more than you think.

19. Copy and paste your "Product Description Page" into the space provided.

20. If you haven't already, be sure to save the input you just provided as you followed the steps above.

Now, that you've developed your page, you're next focus is shipping your product to an Amazon FBA Warehouse and getting your product live and in Active Status. When you're ready, move forward!

Sending Your Product To Your FBA Warehouse

At this point, your product page is ready, so when it becomes active (live) you can maximize your early sales potential. To become active, you first need to focus on printing shipping labels.

It is important to acknowledge that I am assuming you're taking my suggestion of having your supplier send the units to your home or office location. If you're planning on sending the shipment directly from the supplier to the FBA Warehouse, then I recommend you reach out to logisticsplus.net to organize this. My second assumption is that you're sourcing your product from outside the US. If you're sourcing your product from inside the US, then this process will be very simple. Please remember, that for your first order it is important that you see your product units, and assess the quality yourself. You could seriously jeopardize your momentum, and sales potential if you start selling your product, and you get a couple negative reviews.

Side note, negative reviews are inevitable, but they should be the clear minority. We'll discuss strategies to handle negative reviews later on.

Regardless of the location you choose to ship from, here are the steps for printing out your shipping labels, and obtaining your warehouse addresses. Notice the plurality of the word "addresses." Depending on the size of your shipment, Amazon will likely provide you with multiple locations to ship to. This is very common, and they do this so they can strategically place their supply of inventory. They spread it out through the country, so they can more efficiently ship products to a customer.

1. Log into your sellercentral.amazon.com account.

2. Scroll over "Inventory" and click on "Manage Inventory."

3. Click on the down arrow next to "Actions" towards the left of the table.

4. Click on "Send/Replenish Inventory."

5. Select "Create a New Shipping Plan."

6. Complete the "Ship From" information based on where you're shipping from.

7. Select "Case-packed Products" then press "Continue to Shipping Plan."

8. Enter in the amount of units per case, and the amount of cases, and then press "Continue."

9. Select "Amazon" under "Who labels?" - this will cost you $.20 per unit, but I strongly urge that it is worth it.

10. Press "Continue."

11. Press "Approve Shipments."

12. Under "Shipping Service" - select "Small Parcel Deliver" (SPD) and "Amazon-Partnered Carrier" (UPS).

13. Under "Shipment Packing" - enter the total number of boxes. You're going to do this for each warehouse because this will enable you to generate the appropriate amount of shipping labels

14. Enter the box weight and box dimensions. If you don't have these items yet, ask your supplier for the information.

15. Click "Calculate."

16. Select "I agree to the terms and conditions" then press "Accept Charges."

17. Press the "Print Box Labels" button

18. Tape your labels to your boxes and either take them to a UPS store or schedule a UPS pick up at <u>ups.com</u>

Before moving on, it is important to point out that there will be other more efficient options as you scale up your business, but the above steps are for the person just starting out. Always feel free to check out <u>zoniversity.com,</u> which is solely focused on helping people find success on Amazon. Lastly, before you send your units to the FBA Warehouses, it is important to keep 5 to 10 units in case a customer receives a faulty product. You'll be able to provide "Above and Beyond" customer service by overnighting a new product to the customer. Doing so can convert what would be a negative customer experience to an interaction that is more likely to generate a positive review.

Active vs. Inactive Status

This topic does not require a significant amount of attention. However, if it is ignored it can lead to some confusion. After you set up your product page, and everything looks beautiful (or at least good enough to start), your product will not be live. In other words, your product will not be active. Do not panic. Your product will become active once your shipment arrives at the selected warehouses. Amazon will select the warehouses for you. Shipping labels will be generated, and printed by you. Then either sent to your supplier, or applied by you. After this, your product is ready to be shipped from your home or office.

Side note, though I do plan on going further into shipping your units to the warehouse, it is important that you realize for your first order, I recommend all the units be sent to you directly. This way you can do a quality assurance check. I do this for any shipment of 1,000 units or less. The only reason why I don't inspect orders over 1,000 is my disdain for taking the time to physically place the shipping label on the boxes myself. If you're purchasing an amount greater than 1,000 units on your first order then you're taking unnecessary risk.

Refocusing, once your page becomes active that means it is now possible for a person to visit Amazon, and find your product. Please realize that because the page is active, it doesn't mean it's going to be all over the place in front of every shopper. There will be strategies discussed later on to get your page in front of the eyes of plenty of potential customers.

To determine whether or not your product is active or inactive, login to your Seller Central Account, and follow the steps below:

1. Click on "Inventory" towards the top left.

2. Select "Manage Inventory."

3. Look in the column titled "Status."

Side note, if you sell out and don't restock quickly enough, then your product page will automatically become inactive. This is very bad, and should be avoided whenever possible. This can set you back on your keyword rankings. Don't throw away your hard work and persistence working up your keyword rankings only to sell out, have your product become inactive, and essentially have to start over at square one.

<u>Your Product Is Live! Now What?</u>

Key Information

Congratulations! Your product is live! You officially have all of the hard work behind you, and you're closer than ever to generating a consistent source of income. Unfortunately, being live does not ensure sales. Your focus now is climbing the keyword rankings for your top keywords, which is where your product ranks based on the specific term searched. For example, if you sell garbage bags maybe one of your main keywords is "tall kitchen bags". If somebody were to search that, your page rank would dictate where your product is found on a page, and what page you're on. It goes without saying, ideally your product is the first product on page one (if you get there, then you've struck gold). The eventual goal is to generate consistent, organic sales with little to no marketing costs by getting as high of a page ranking as possible for multiple keywords. Again, you should be using <u>merchantwords.com</u> as a resource to help you prioritize your keywords. To achieve this you need to consider a few factors:

<u>Seller Feedback</u> - This is the social proof that you are a reliable seller. Similar to the "Product Reviews" your "Seller Feedback" is out of a possible 5 points. This is not supposed to be a review of the product. For example, if a customer were not satisfied with the date that they received the product, then they might leave negative feedback.

<u>Product Reviews</u> - This is the social proof that your product is of a high quality, and is what the advertising says it is going to be. One example of how I accidentally prompted negative reviews is that I offered a free eBook with purchase, but my email account with the attachment wasn't working for a while, before I realized it. The email that contained the eBook was not being sent out, and I received two negative reviews that stated the product was high quality, but they were still waiting on the eBook.

Unit Session Percentage - This is what I (and many) refer to as your conversion rate. In other words, how many people who visit your page actually make a purchase. A unit session could be equal to 3 page views.

Internally Driven Amazon Traffic - This is all traffic that comes to your page from Amazon. If somebody visits amazon.com, then searches a keyword, and visits your page, then that is traffic to your product page that was from Amazon. This is one example; there are other examples like Amazon PPC (Pay Per Click) that will be covered later on.

Externally Driven Amazon Traffic - This is all traffic that comes to your page from outside of Amazon. If somebody Goggles a keyword, follows a search result to your YouTube video that show how to use your product, and then clicks on a link, that your YouTube video contains, and is taken to your product page, then that is traffic driven from outside Amazon. This is one example; there are other examples, like Facebook ads, that will be covered later on.

This is a lot to take in, but it is extremely important that you understand each of the above items. They're important, because they'll guide your decision-making when you begin to strategize how you want to position your product. Later on, we'll discuss how to use the above information to help increase sales of your product.

Before moving on, it is important to note that nobody knows for sure which of the above factors, or other existing factors, are most important.

In the very early stages, focus on obtaining product reviews. Moreover, plan to take a loss on your first 20 to 50 units, to obtain positive reviews. If you choose not to do this, you can still do okay. However, you're going to end up spending more on marketing, because you won't have the social proof to increase your page ranking for your selected keywords. Either way, you're going to have to plan on making a minor investment to get your product where it needs to be. The more you're willing to wait out the profits, and reinvest your earnings into your product, the bigger the payoffs down the road. I'm not saying you won't be able to take a profit early on, but your growth will likely be minimal, and your rankings will probably be pretty volatile, and provide a less consistent source of income.

Marketing Your Product

If you have been reading this book as a guide, and have been completing the steps provided as you go, then you should be extremely proud of yourself. The majority of people, no matter how structured and laid out a plan is, will quit due to a lack of endurance. The reality is, earning passive income isn't easy.

Side note, this does not have to be passive income. You can make it a legitimate, full time business. Many people already do. However, you should know that if you have a full time job and/or a family, you have completed the legwork. Now you are in a slower, strategic phase. As a husband and father of two with a full time job, I remember yearning to be proud of myself for sacrificing hours upon hours to eventually receive passive income. Congratulations! You are there. Now you need to focus on generating sales.

Generating Sales

This part of the book will provide a basic strategy, and other avenues to research, that will almost certainly ignite your sales. However, please know that there are plenty more strategies out there, and as e-commerce evolves there are new strategies that will be born. As I sell products myself, any strategies I use and/or learn about will certainly find their way onto zoniversity.com.

Also, the only real way to stick this process out is to adapt to any change that you encounter. For that reason, I invite you to join my private Facebook group where you can collaborate and reach out to likeminded people going through the same process. To join, search AmazonSalesFormula.

Strategy #1 - Amazon Pay Per Click (PPC)

Amazon PPC allows you the opportunity to advertise your product on pages much higher than you'll start out on. They're easy to create, and you can limit your spending by setting a rule that will not allow your daily spending over a maximum amount. Before the specific steps are provided, there are multiple general points to recognize.

You need to...

Have a strategy to determine your strongest keywords (I use merchantwords.com).

Approach this as a test process. When you have a minute or two look at how your keywords are performing. Are your clicks converting to sales? Are your keywords too specific? Are they too broad? There is no set answer to these questions. Take a small amount of time every once and awhile (more often if you have a high daily maximum spending amount) to analyze your data.

Get creative! A keyword term may not be searched a ton, but if it converts at a high percentage, then you might have found something that your competition has overlooked.

Think about uses for your product that are outside of the obvious. Then develop an experimental list of keywords based on those uses. The good news is, you can set your maximum bid price to whatever you want. This way you don't have to worry about a surprise click that costs you $10 per click.

Sticking with the $10 click example, if you bid $10 per click on a keyword, and the next highest bid is $.88, you will land your product on the front page for that keyword, and you will only pay $.89 per click. In other words, you will only pay $.01 more than the next bid amount under yours. Be careful though. If you bid $10 and a competitor bids $10.01, then you'll be charged $10 per click. Unfortunately, you cannot view other sellers' bids. You can only view the average bid price.

Lastly, be open to learning the process. It is simply unneeded, and most likely counterproductive, for me to try to explain every thing I know about Amazon PPC;

read books, find blogs, and join Facebook groups. I'm not saying go crazy acquiring information, because that is the opposite of passive, but take some time every few months or so to check in on this topic.

Shifting gears to more specific steps, view the following items to help you set up an Amazon PPC campaign:

1. Log into your "Seller Central account."

2. Scroll over "Campaign."

3. Click on "Campaign Manager."

4. Click "Create Campaign."

5. Compete the form provided. Do not worry about setting an end date.

6. Click either "Automatic Targeting" or "Manual Targeting."

7. Click "Continue to Next Step" and follow steps beyond that point (it is very straightforward).

Regarding Step 6, I recommend you create two campaigns. One should use Manual Targeting, which means you pick your own keywords, and one should use automatic targeting, which means Amazon will provide suggested keywords. You can then compare your data for each campaign to see which is most effective for you.

Below are additional marketing concepts that are worth looking into, but I'm not delving too deep for a couple of reasons. First, I did not use these methods to start. I focused on only the strategy above, and it was enough to get me to a point I was happy with. Second, too much information will cause analysis paralysis. After you feel as though you have exhausted your Amazon PPC strategies, then I recommend you research the following.

Google/Bing/Yahoo Ads - operates similarly to Amazon PPC, only for people who are searching via Google/Bing/Yahoo.

Facebook Ads - what makes these marketing campaigns stand out is the ability to specifically target your audience. Beware of spending too much, and look for resources that help you establish a Facebook ad. It isn't super complicated, but it isn't simple either.

Bloggers - reach out to bloggers who target an audience that might be interested in purchasing your product. They could review your product, interview you about why you chose that product, etc.

YouTube Videos - film videos that talk about your product, whether it be instructional on how to use it, or just a cool mini commercial. Look at fiverr.com and animoto.com to help you with this process.

Press Releases - use fiverr.com or elance.com to help you write and publish a press release for your product. You can create a promotion. Then publish a press release describing the value and steps to receive the promotion.

To reiterate and close, the additional marketing strategies noted above are certainly worth looking into, but may not be necessary depending on the product you have chosen. Likewise, if you attempt to juggle too many marketing campaigns too early on, then you may find yourself totally confused and overwhelmed.

Keyword Research

The rule of thumb for real estate investment is "location, location, location." The rule of thumb for Amazon sales is "keywords, keywords, keywords". Keywords are utilized in a variety of ways on both the buyer's end and the seller's end. Before going further into this, please note the definition of keyword.

Keyword - a word or phrase utilized to search for an item, product, or topic.

In other words, if you go to Google, and search for something, whatever you type into the search is the keyword. This is how the majority of people find products to purchase on amazon.com. When a person is looking to purchase a hair dryer on Amazon, they don't typically visit the site, and start browsing the beauty products. That would take an excessive amount of time. Instead, they visit Amazon, and in the search bar, they type in "hairdryer". If that person wanted a Conair hairdryer, then they would type that into the search bar, scroll through the first page or two, until they found one that looked interesting. At that point, they would click that item, and either make the purchase or click back, and continue to look.

Your goal is to have your product show up first when people search your related keywords. This is where the research comes into play, because keywords are not created equal. This is where I recommend merchantwords.com. This site is excellent for two reasons: 1.) It is extremely simple and easy to use. 2.) It gives you the amount of times keywords you pick are searched on amazon.com. This is especially important, because people who visit Amazon are looking to make a purchase. Many of your potential customers already have their credit card on file, so they can make a purchase at the click of a button. You want to position your product so it is in the customers' line of sight. To do this, you need your product to rank well for multiple keywords. Follow the steps below to figure out what keywords are going to work best for you. The list of keywords generated from these steps will play a role in multiple ways throughout your product page setup process, and in your marketing strategy.

1. Grab a pen and paper, and start brainstorming a list of as many keywords for your product. Dig deep on this one, and do not limit yourself here. Quantity over quality during this step is a necessity.

2. Use the list you have, and start searching each keyword from your list with merchantwords.com. Be aware that this is a paid site, but it is a nominal monthly fee, and very well worth the cost. If you prefer not to spend the money, then go to google.com and type in "Google keyword planner". You'll have to set up an account, but it won't cost you anything. Please note that merchantwords.com has proven to be much more telling of what potential customers are searching for on amazon.com.

3. Click on the down arrow next to "Sort by" and select "Highest Search Volume First".

4. Start making a list, use a spreadsheet of some sort for all the keywords that are related to your product, and that have significant search volume. The higher the number the better. I can't provide a minimum number, because it really depends on how competitive your product

is. If you're thinking of moving forward with a product that has a bunch of similar products with a significant amount of reviews, then you want a higher number of searches. To help yourself later on, set up two columns for your list. One column should include the keywords, and the column next to it should have the amount of searches.

5. Go through your list one more time, and eliminate any words that are too much of a reach in terms of how closely related the keywords are to your product. This may be a product that has a ton of searches, but the reality is, you want people who are looking for your product, not seeing your product as they look for something else.

6. Once you've eliminated words that aren't closely related enough, order your list by search volume. Only do this step if it is easy for you. Doing it won't save you more than 5 to 10 minutes, so if it takes you longer than that, don't worry about it.

Keep this list handy. As it was stated earlier, this list will be utilized to help you in multiple ways throughout the process of selling your product. You may not realize it, but this process is market research. In other words, if all of your keywords are generating very little to zero searches, then you need to ask yourself if you're venturing into the right market.

One more note on this process. Don't let the appeal of a niche product cause you to avoid high volume searched products. The reality is, both niche products and high demand products can work out in your favor.

View it this way; take a large piece of the small pie, or a small piece of the large pie. Either combination can lead to significant sales if approached wisely and strategically.

Understanding and Obtaining Product Reviews

You've now established a market-entry marketing plan. Next you'll need to maximize your unit session percentage conversions. To do this you'll need to obtain reviews. Before we focus on strategies to obtain reviews, it is important to discuss the two forms of reviews: verified reviews and unverified reviews.

Verified Reviews are reviews that are made by people who purchased your product through Amazon (some people sell their products at farmers markets, eBay, newegg.com, etc.). The customers who purchase a product via Amazon, then leave a product review will leave a verified review. There is nothing that you or the customer needs to do to make it verified. It will automatically say that it is a verified review.

Unverified Reviews are reviews made by people who have made a purchase on Amazon within the last six months, but haven't purchased your product through Amazon. These people have the option of leaving a review, but the credibility is minimized, as it will not say verified review under the name. There is a belief, though it is nowhere in writing, that unverified reviews help you significantly less then verified reviews as far as page ranking is concerned.

In addition to Verified Reviews being more valuable than Unverified Reviews, I would also say that to the observant shopper it might appear fraudulent if your product has an excessive amount of Unverified Reviews. That said, I initially had my friends and family members leave me a total of 12 unverified reviews. My logic was that 12 unverified reviews looked better than zero reviews.

Once you begin selling your product consistently, I recommend you stay away from unverified reviews. In fact, I would focus the majority of my efforts on obtaining verified reviews from family members and friends to start the momentum. Below is a strategy to obtain verified reviews when your product is live, but not selling consistently.

1. Write a list of all of your friends and family members that have Amazon accounts.

2. Reach out to each person on the list, tell them about what you're doing, and politely ask for support.

3. For each yes you receive send them an email with directions. Provide a link directly to your product.

4. Each person should make a purchase using a promo code that you create. The promo code should allow the person to purchase the item for a $1.00. Check out zoniversity.com if you need help creating a promotion.

5. Follow up with each person via email to ensure that they provided their review. Be polite and respectful, and accept the fact that some people will tell you that they're going to, and they never will.

Be aware that the steps above will cost you money. If you provide a promotion that sells your product for $1.00, you will take a loss. If you are uncomfortable with this, or do not/ cannot make the investment, then follow steps one through three above. Instead of step four, you're going to skip to step five. If you're confused by this, then check out zoniversity.com for templates you can use to help guide the email that you send to friends and family who you're requesting reviews from.

Here is another strategy if you don't want to use the promotional code option.

1. Write a list of all of your friends and family members that have Amazon accounts.

2. Reach out to each person on the list, tell them about what you're doing and politely ask for support.

3. For each yes you receive send them an email with instructions that ask for their address. Be sure to explain why you're requesting their address because this is personal information.

4. Mail or in some way provide an Amazon gift card to that person in a handwritten thank you card. Thank them for the support and explain how helpful their being.

5. Send an email as a follow up to ensure that they leave the review.

The strategy above can cost some money as well, and the total amount depends on how many gift cards you choose to purchase. What makes the strategy effective is that the Amazon gift card and the thank you card serve as both a reminder, and a tiny bit of a guilt trip for those that aren't following through. Most people can't accept a thank you card for something they didn't do. Is it guaranteed? No. The success rate depends on the people you're dealing with, but it can be very effective.

A third option, I would suggest is some type of review website program. Before I go any further though, you should know that this is technically a gray area, and Amazon does not like sites that offer reviews. However, they can really spike your movement in page ranks. Check out zonblast.com.

The final option I am going to provide is reaching out to Amazon's top reviewers at http://www.amazon.com/review/top-reviewers. Approach this at your own risk. Some reviewers can be very tough, and a negative review early on can hurt the growth of your product ranking. Be sure to read many of the reviews by a person you're thinking about asking to review your product. If the person has a high amount of negative reviews, you'll want to avoid that person.

When, and if, you do decide to contact some reviewers, be sure to ask them how they'd like the process to be facilitated. In other words, do they want a promo code, a gift card, or the product itself (which would in turn make their review unverified)?

To close this section, it is important to reiterate one thought. In the beginning the name of the game is obtaining reviews and maintaining a high conversion rate. There will be more on maintaining a high conversion rate, but the information above should give you plenty to start obtaining reviews.

Automatic Emails vs. Manual Emails

As you know by now, product reviews and customer feedback play a crucial role in earning and maintaining sales. In order to maximize product reviews, you need to contact your customers.

This might sound simple, but Amazon views your customers as their customers, and they do not want buyers to be inundated by third party retailers (which is what you are in this case) every time they make a purchase on amazon.com.

This translates to Amazon not allowing you to view your customer's email addresses. If you were hoping to build an email list out of your customer's information, it won't be as straightforward as you might of hoped. There is, however, an opportunity to contact your customers. Follow the instructions below to send a manual email to a customer.

1. Log into your "Seller Central account."

2. Click on "Orders."

3. Click on "Manage Orders."

4. Click on the name next to "Contact Buyer."

5. Insert your message into the box (4,000-character limit).

Two points of emphasis for the above instructions. First, this is to send emails manually. This means for each and every customer that purchases your product, you're going to have to complete this process. Second, step five states that you should insert your message. The word insert is used instead of write, because you should have a few templates saved and ready to copy/paste into the box to help generate these emails more efficiently. I recommend you send each customer no less than three emails, and no more than four emails (depending on what you write). Speaking of which, when you write your email templates follow the pointers below.

1. Use the customer's first name.

2. Be happy, funny, and light.

3. Keep it quick.

4. No more than three sentences per paragraph.

5. No more than two paragraphs.

6. Be grateful. This person just purchased your product.

7. When requesting a review use the attached link:

    a. http://www.amazon.com/review/create-review/ref=cm_cr_dp_wrt_summary?ie=UTF 8&asin={Insert your ASIN Here}

    b. Your ASIN can be found by logging into your Seller Account, clicking Inventory then viewing the fourth column titled "ASIN/ISBN"

8. Provide a couple tips to maximize your product's value.

If you'd like to see and use specific templates check out zoniversity.com. Before moving on, please note the red font in the review link above. Be sure to insert your ASIN, which you can find by logging into to your "Seller

Central account." Click on "Inventory, then "Manage Inventory." Next to your product name, you'll see your ASIN. Copy and paste right where it says, "Insert your ASIN Here".

All of that said, if the goal is to scale a business, and generate a significant amount of passive income, then sending manual emails is a bit of a contradiction. When I initially started selling my own products on Amazon, my goal was to generate passive income. I never sent manual emails with the exception of a couple specific displeased customers.

I always went with automatic emails. To do this, you'll need to reach out to a third party that connects to your Seller Central account, and sends emails automatically for you (once you provide the templates). There are many options out there that can be easily found through a Google search. I recommend www.feedbackfive.com. They're affordable for a person starting out who doesn't have a ton of sales, and they make the process fairly simple and straightforward.

If you want to generate income while your business is running on co-pilot, then you're definitely going to need to look into automated emails. Don't feel like you have to resolve this before you start selling. Setup does not take long. I would focus on generating consistent sales, and once you hit your limit sending manual emails, you can make the switch to automatic.

<u>Conclusion</u>

You've done it. You have successfully identified an in demand product with brand potential, created your own brand, sourced a product under your own brand, leveraged the FBA process, and began marketing your product and brand. You should be proud of yourself. Be sure to take a minute every once and awhile to recognize what you have accomplished. If you haven't already, you now fall into a category of a very small group of people who can generate passive income.

Before I let you go, I want to make a couple of points that hopefully keep you focused, and point you in a direction that leads you to great success. First, I know everybody's financial situation is different, but the more you invest on the front end the greater profits you'll receive on the back end. Second, successful completion of the steps and strategies provided in this book means you have a passive revenue stream. I recommend you tweak one detail of your page or offering (price, product image, order of words in title, etc.) a day until you start averaging a conversion rate of 20% or higher. Third, the book has concluded, but you are not alone. If you encounter obstacles I hope you view <u>zoniversity.com</u> and my Facebook group AmazonSalesFormula as resources you can count on. Lastly, always feel free to email me at <u>mike@zoniversity.com</u>. I will make every effort to reply with helpful and effective resources, and information.

All the best and good luck!

47008064R00050

Made in the USA
Middletown, DE
14 August 2017